It Happened in Little Valley

A Case Study of Uxoricide

Max Malikow

It Happened in Little Valley

Copyright © 2016 by Max Malikow

Published by:
Theocentric Publishing Group
1069A Main Street
Chipley, Florida 32428

www.theocentricpublishing.com

Library of Congress Control Number: 2016961800

ISBN 9780986405594

Acknowledgments

Had I never met Ralph Riggs, the son of Ralph and Sue Ann Riggs, the events of November 28, 1956 and following would have remained restricted to newspaper accounts, police reports, and court records. His willingness to share with me all he had accumulated and everything he could remember about his mother's untimely death made what I have written possible. Ralph's sister, Kristie Yunker, also contributed to the retelling of this story. Little Valley Town Historian Ryan West provided information I could not have acquired without his assistance. Finally, a collateral benefit of my research was that it led me to Ira Joe Fisher, who recalled this story from his childhood. His willingness to share what he remembered is appreciated.

Table of Contents

Introduction

There was surely nothing to indicate at the time that such evidently small incidents would render whole dreams forever irredeemable.

-Kazuo Ishiguro, *The Remains of the Day*

The murder of Sue Ann Riggs by her husband, Ralph Riggs, and subsequent suicide of her lover, Albert Roy Marsh, were the culmination of ordinary people engaged in ordinary circumstances. Ralph and Sue had a troubled marriage; Albert had recently divorced; Sue and Albert were having an affair. These circumstances hardly constitute a perfect storm for tragedy, but tragedy occurred in the early morning of November 28, 1956 in Little Valley, New York, the ordinary village in which they lived. Little Valley, population 1,200 then as now, is north of Salamanca and south of Mansfield, two other unexceptional communities. The nearest city of appreciable size is Olean, where Ralph Riggs was employed as a draftsman. It was from there he returned home unexpectedly to find Albert Marsh hiding in a bedroom closet. Troubled marriages, divorces, and affairs, although unfavorable, are commonplace. Even when they converge they rarely culminate in a homicide or suicide and even less often both.

It was in the spring of 2016 when I became interested in the intersection of these three lives. It was then that I met the son of Ralph Riggs, who was three-years-old at the time of his mother's murder. She was holding him and his year-and-a-half old sister, Kristie, when their father fired three bullets from a .32 caliber pistol into their mother's head. What started as mere curiosity on my part soon became the subject of intense research. I found myself wanting to know more as I learned more. The explanation for this unexpected development is my recognition that this is a story about all of us. Not because murder and suicide invade and profoundly affect each of our lives, but because the conditions that existed in the lives of Ralph, his wife, and her lover are familiar to us all, albeit with different results. These conditions are not getting the life we dreamed of or even envisioned; miscalculating what is necessary for our happiness; and taking actions that produce unintended consequences for others, including those we love. Moreover, although not every life is radically reordered by a tragedy, each of us is aware that none of us is exempt from a personal cataclysm.

In addition, this story is a real-life instantiation of three realities we grow to recognize as a part of life. One, the law of unintended consequences is inescapable. Sue did not anticipate her affair would end in a homicide, but it did. Albert did not intend that Sue would be murdered by her husband, but she was. Two, every tragedy leaves in its wake unspeakable heartbreak. This is unambiguously clear from a letter Sue's mother wrote in 1988, 32 years after Sue's death. Three, even people we know can surprise us by acting out of character. Those who knew Ralph were shocked by what he did. Whatever Ralph intended while driving home that morning, it was not putting a gun to his wife's head and pulling the trigger.

Assigning responsibility for any incident that involves more than one person is no easy matter. The law of cause-and-effect complicates the task of apportioning blame for Sue's murder. Not only did she choose to engage in an affair, but she also chose to remain with an abusive husband who was given to excessive drinking. Albert persisted in the affair in spite of three previous encounters with Ralph, who warned him to stay away from his wife. On the night of the murder Ralph chose to drink profusely and exercise poor judgment by driving 28 miles from Olean to Little Valley, arriving home unanticipated by his wife. (Earlier Ralph told Sue he would remain in Olean if he had too much to drink.) Sue and Albert's contributions to this calamity notwithstanding, it was Ralph who committed murder. Hence, the assessment of the renown psychiatrist

Introduction

Scott Peck applies to Ralph: "Triggers are pulled by individuals. In the last analysis, every single human act is ultimately the result of an individual choice" (1983, p. 215). Since all the unintended consequences of an action cannot be known with certainty, one way of determining responsibility is to reduce it to the principles of knowability and foreseeability. The former means even if all the ramifications of an action cannot be known, the legality or morality of that action is knowable. The latter speaks to what a reasonable person can anticipate as a possible, if not a probable, consequence of that action. Regarding knowability, Sue and Albert knew adultery to be morally wrong. Concerning foreseeability, it is doubtful that Ralph, Sue or Albert anticipated a homicide. However, Ralph is responsible for spouse abuse. Two 1954 domestic disturbance police reports include him having physically abused Sue. Ralph is responsible for his contribution to the deterioration of his marriage, which presaged the affair.

In the present case it is tempting to speculate about hypotheticals: What if Ralph had spent the night in Olean? What if he had been stopped by the police for driving under the influence of alcohol? What if he had not found Albert hiding under a blanket in a bedroom closet? Answering any of these questions is beyond human capability.

It Happened in Little Valley

This lamentable event of 60 years ago is a human story. Not because it is a story about these three people, but because it is a story about all people. More often than not, when extraordinary occurrences happen they happen to ordinary people. Moreover, with very few exceptions, the life of one person affects the lives of others. The poet John Donne recognized this and wrote:

> No man is an island,
> Entire of itself,
> Every man is a piece of the continent,
> A part of the main.
> If a clod be washed away by the sea,
> Europe is the less. ...
> Any man's death diminishes me,
> Because I am involved in mankind,
> And therefore never send to know for whom the bell tolls;
> It tolls for thee (1624).

Chapter I. The Murder

Murder is born of love, and love attains its greatest intensity in murder.

- Octave Mirbeau

Sue Riggs and Albert Marsh had an evening and night of availability to each other on November 28, 1956 - or so they thought. In his statement to the police, Marsh said he went to the Riggs home at around 4 p.m., left at approximately 6:30 p.m., and returned at about 9 p.m. Upon returning, he and Sue watched television for about two hours and then went upstairs to her bedroom where they lay in bed reading. At approximately midnight Ralph called Sue from Olean. They spoke briefly and she returned to bed and told Albert that Ralph had been drinking. Albert and Sue continued reading in bed until a few minutes before 2 a.m. when they heard someone banging on the door. Suspecting it was Ralph, Albert hid in the bedroom closet while Sue went downstairs to see who was at the door. It was Ralph.

There is no inconsistency between the statements Albert Marsh and Ralph Riggs made to the police. Ralph reported that he arrived home at approximately 1:55 a.m. and became suspicious when it took Sue so long to come to the door. Upon entering, he searched the downstairs while Sue returned to their upstairs bedroom. When asked, "Had you ever found company in your house with your wife before?" he answered:

> Yes, three times, once while we lived on Park Place in Little Valley in 1955, in August or September, I came home and found Albert Marsh, Jr. in the house with my wife Sue. I told Marsh to get out of my house and to stay out and that we did not need him around there (11/28/56).

When asked about the other two occasions Ralph responded:

> One time in the evening I came into the house and found Sue lying on the couch with Albert Marsh, Jr. sitting on the couch. Both were fully clothed and I did not do anything beyond telling them both to get out of the house and to be out of the house when I returned. I returned about 9 p.m. and Marsh was gone and Sue was still there. Sue and I had words but nothing more came of it (11/28/56).

Concerning the third occasion, he recounted:

One night, about midnight or later, I came home and found Sue and Marsh in the house. I fought with Marsh that night and gave him a black eye and choked my wife some and then stopped and called the Sheriff's office and then Marsh left (11/28/56).

Albert Marsh's statement to the police was given the same morning Ralph gave his statement. In it he described what happened after Ralph returned home and found Albert there:

I stepped in the closet in her bedroom and she went downstairs and let him in. It sounded like he came upstairs and then he went downstairs again and then came back upstairs again. He opened the closet door and saw me and hit me a couple of times. I tried to reason with him and then I went downstairs. I don't know if he came downstairs before or after me, and she also came downstairs. I heard her arguing with him as I unlocked the back door. I went out the back door and through the garage and out the driveway. I could see Ralph Riggs through the kitchen window. I went to the

Chapter I. The Murder

Rock City Hotel where I have room number 27 (11/28/56).

Ralph described his discovery of Albert hiding under a blanket in the bedroom closet:

> I grabbed a hold of the blanket and under it was Albert Marsh, Jr. I started away from him and then turned around hit him a couple of times with my fist and we wrestled around in the closet and into my bedroom. Sue was sitting up in bed yelling for me to stop and telling me to think of the children. I told Sue I would go down and get the gun. I went downstairs and Marsh was still upstairs (11/28/56).

Ralph went to the gun cabinet in the dining room. When he had difficulty unlocking it he broke the cabinet's glass window with his fist and retrieved a .32 caliber Savage automatic pistol and loaded three shells into the chamber. While he was doing this Sue went to her son's bedroom and took Little Ralph and Kristie in her arms. She was crying, holding one child in each arm when Ralph entered the room and said, "I ought to shoot you." He described the last moments of Sue's life to Sheriff Morgan Sigel with these words:

> I had the gun pointed at Sue and I talked to her, I do not remember what was said. She had her head down and I pointed the pistol at the back of her head and pulled the trigger three times. I went out the back door and looked for Albert Marsh and did not find him. I had thrown the pistol on the couch and I found it and put four shells in it and took Ralph and Kristie upstairs and put them to bed and then called the Sheriff's office and told them I had shot my wife (11/28/56).

Ralph then hid the gun in the cellar, turned off all the lights in the house, retrieved the gun, got into his car, drove around the block, and returned home. He parked in the driveway, locked the car doors, and lay on the floor in front of the front seat. He remained there until a sheriff broke a window, unlocked a door, and took Ralph into custody.

The Irish writer and politician Sir Richard Steele wrote, "The married state is the compleatest image of heaven and hell we are capable of receiving in this life" (Viorst, 1986, p. 202). Concerning marriage, the poet and author Judith Viorst has written,

Chapter I. The Murder

Our friends are less than perfect. We accept their imperfections and pride ourselves on our sense of reality. But when it comes to love we stubbornly cling to our illusions - to conscious and unconscious visions of how things should be. When it comes to love - to romantic love and sexual love and married love - we have to learn again, with difficulty, how to let go of all kinds of expectations (1986, p. 202).

The marriage of Ralph and Sue Riggs had deteriorated to a state of far less than either expected when they married in April of 1953. The year prior to the murder they separated briefly (approximately three weeks). In 1954 the police intervened on two occasions in response to complaints of domestic disturbance that included Sue having been physically abused by Ralph. The September 4, 1954 report of Sheriff Joseph Mongillo reads:

> I located Sue's husband Ralph at the Fair Grounds and took both he and Sue to Judge Weed. Judge Weed talked to both of them and convinced them to settle their difficulties outside of court. Both agreed to this and went home (09/04/54).

Chapter II. The Suicide

Who can stop grief's avalanche once it starts to roll?

- Euripides, *Medea*

Albert Roy Marsh, Jr. was born April 9, 1932 in East Randolph, New York, ten miles west of Little Valley, where his life ended 24 years later. He committed suicide twenty hours after the murder of Sue Riggs, shooting himself in the head with a .22 caliber rifle. He did this in the parking lot of the funeral home where Sue's body lay in preparation for her funeral.

Marsh was dressed in a freshly pressed dark blue suit. Beside his body was a note which read:

"I am sorry I have to do this. Life without Sue is nothing."

On the car seat was a florist's box with (a) spray of roses. On the box was written: "These roses are for Sue" (*Salamanca Republican-Press*, 11/29/1956).

Albert was voted "Best All-Around Athlete" in the Randolph Central High School class of 1950, having played three years of basketball and two years of football. Divorced, he left behind a son, Steven, age five, a daughter, Jean Marie, age three, and a son, David, age one. A fourth child, Craig, died in a drowning at age two in 1952. Albert Marsh, Jr. was laid to rest in the East Randolph/Maple Hills Cemetery, next to Craig. Twenty-two years later, they were joined by Albert Marsh, Sr.

Understanding Suicide

Why did Albert Marsh commit suicide? His suicide note communicated despair at the prospect of life without Sue. Among the many aphorisms used by mental health professionals to characterize suicide is, "Suicide is a permanent solution to a temporary problem." Had he given himself a few days or even a day to begin to acclimate to his pain, he might not have taken his life. Edwin Shneidman, long recognized as an authority on suicide, has written about the impulsivity of many suicides:

> Suicide involves both inner disturbance and the idea of
> death as an escape. But it is simply good sense not to
> commit an irrevocable suicide during a transient
> perturbation in the mind. Suicide is not the thing to do

when you are disturbed and your thinking is constricted. There is a short aphorism or maxim that captures this life saving truth: Never kill yourself while you are suicidal. You can, if you must, think about suicide as much as your mind wishes and let the thought of suicide - the possibility that you could do it - carry you through the dark night. Night after night, day after day, until the thought of self-destruction runs its course, and a fresh view of your own frustrated needs comes into clearer focus in your mind and you can, at last, pursue the realistic aspects, however dire, of your natural life (1996, p. 166).

Seventy-five percent of accomplished suicides occur without a written, parting thought from the deceased (Jamison, 1999, p. 75). Moreover, even among the one in four suicides that is accompanied by a note, "it is unclear if these notes represent the emotional states, motivations, and experiences of those who leave behind a written record" (p. 75). Albert's note made no mention of guilt for having been involved with another man's wife or the fatal consequence of that involvement. Neither was there a hint of survivor guilt for having escaped the fate that Ralph inflicted upon Sue.

Chapter II. The Suicide

The only other document provided by Albert is his statement to Sheriff Sigel, given the day of the murder. It included no mention of despair at the thought of life without Sue or guilt for having been her lover. It provided no indication of his imminent suicide. Nevertheless, it is reasonable to infer from the events of November 28, 1956 that guilt contributed to Albert's self-administered execution.

John Maltsberger, a psychiatrist and past President of the American Association of Suicidology, summarized why people commit suicide in a terse statement: "People commit suicide not because of anger, but rage; not because of depression, but despair; not because of loneliness, but aloneness" (1987). Arguably, Albert's suicide was driven by despair - a despair derived from the anticipation of a life without Sue and a life of unremitting guilt for having survived the relationship that brought her life to an end.

Shneidman has written of the restricted thinking of people in despair who isolate themselves.

Every single instance of suicide is an action by the dictator or emperor of your mind. But in every case of suicide, the person is getting bad advice from a part of that mind, the inner chamber of councilors, who are in a temporary panicked state and in no position to serve the person's best long-range interests. Then it is time to reach outside your own imperial head and seek more qualified and measured advice from others who, out of loyalty to your larger social self, will throw in on the side of life, and - to use a Japanese image - will urge the chrysanthemum, not the sword (1996, pp. 165-166).

The poet Mary Karr had the same tendency of suicidal people in mind when she wrote "Incant Against Suicide:"

Buy neither gun nor blue-edged blade.

Avoid green rope, high windows, rat poison, cobra pits, and the long vanishing point of those train tracks that draw you to horizon's razor.

Only this way will another day refine you. (Natural death's no oxymoron.)

Your head's a bad neighborhood. Don't go there alone, even if you have to stop strangers to ask the way (2001, p. 3).

If Albert Marsh spoke to no one between the end of his statement to Sheriff Sigel and his suicide then he spent the last hours of his life alone in the "bad neighborhood" about which Mary Karr cautioned. This would mean he spent his last hours recycling self-destructive thoughts with neither challenge nor intervention. This unobstructed momentum toward the imagined relief of death culminated in the act that added his three children to three others who already had been consigned to the permanent loss of a parent.

Constricted thinking drove Albert to estimate his feelings for the rest of his life from how he felt in the 20 hours between Sue's death and his own. Part of this tragic story is Albert's projection that how he felt in the wake of her death was how he would feel for as long as he lived.

Aaron Ben-Zeev, author of *In the Name of Love: Romantic Ideology and Its Victim*, offers an interesting observation concerning suicide and unreciprocated love:

Committing suicide because of unrequited love is not an unusual story; some even regard it as a perfect manifestation of true love. As a result of unrequited love, men commit suicide three to four times more than women, and it is virtually only men who kill their partners when the latter leave or intend to leave them. In this sense, women are more realistic; they tend to be more accepting of the fact that love might not endure forever (2014, p. 5).

epublican-Press

TEMPERATURES
High for 6 hours ending at noon, 46, 2 and 3 a.m., low, 30, 9 and 10 p.m., year ago, 6 to 22.

Y., THURSDAY, NOVEMBER 29, 1956

Single Copies Five Cents

U.N. · **ngary** · **vers**

'Other Man' Kills Self In LV Triangle Slaying

Iraq's Premier Firmly at Post

Campaign to Discredit Government Mounts

By WILLIAM L. RYAN

BAGHDAD, Iraq. — Iraq's Premier Nuri Said is reported standing firm against a mounting campaign aimed at discrediting his government. The controlling pro-Nuri army clique in Syria and the Egyptian government are believed sponsoring the campaign.

Khalid Ibrahim, Iraqi information director, declared the Premier has no intention of quitting his post or making changes in his Cabinet "for the time being."

The Baghdad military governor broadcast an appeal to the people urging them to be calm and not to yield to "subversive elements," which the government says are trying to incite widespread demonstrations.

Nuri's government denied reports that dozens of persons have been killed and wounded in Iraq's main cities. It reiterated that only two civilians were killed and some police and civilians wounded in a clash in the holy Moslem city of Najaf, in southwest Iraq.

Damascus Radio declared 101 Iraqis were killed in four days of anti-government demonstrations in Najaf. It asserted the "victims fell by police fire" as they protested against Nuri's government and demanded support for Egypt. Iraq has accused Syria of waging a campaign of subversion against the Nuri government. Syria has charged Iraq with seeking to undermine the governments of both Syria and Jordan. Egyptian President Nasser is believed supporting the Syrians in the Syrian-Iraqi dispute.

In Damascus, the Syrian Foreign Ministry issued a statement affirming Syria's "positive neutrality" between the East and West. Echoing recent Moscow Radio broadcasts, it charged "imperialistic propaganda" was preparing the way for an eventual attack on the Arab world.

ALBERT ROY MARSH JR.

Nation's Traffic Death Toll Drops

12 Per Cent Slump Is Called 'Amazing'

CHICAGO — The nation's traffic death toll has taken a sharp drop — a turn the National Safety Council calls "amazing."

The council reported today that fatalities slumped 12 per cent in October.

It stated that the abrupt downturn:

Halted a rise that had extended through 19 consecutive months.

Completely reversed the normal seasonal trend.

Set up a chance to keep this 1956 total from reaching record heights.

Deaths on the streets and roads in October numbered 3,400. That was 12 per cent under the number died in October, 1955. It was the lowest toll for any October since 1949.

"Not since January of 1948," the council said, "had traffic deaths dropped so sharply."

Albert Marsh Shoots Self at Funeral Home

LITTLE VALLEY — The "other man" in a fatal love triangle took his own life here last night, just twenty hours after the pistol murder of a Little Valley housewife.

Albert Roy Marsh Jr., twenty-four, of East Randolph, inflicted fatal wounds shot himself to death about 10 o'clock last night in the parking lot of a funeral home here.

Inside the funeral home lay the body of Mrs. Sue Ann Sharpe Riggs, twenty-four, mother of three small children, who was shot to death at 2 a.m. yesterday after her husband came home to find Marsh hiding in a closet.

The husband, Ralph Riggs, twenty-four, a draftsman for Clark Bros. Co. in Olean, is in Cattaraugus County Jail, held for first-degree murder in his wife's death.

Roses and Note on Seat

A spray of twenty-five red roses "for Sue" and a despondent note lay on the car seat beside Marsh's body when it was found at the rear of the Vandenwerker Funeral Home, 411 Rock City St., where Marsh at times had helped out as a driver.

Sheriff Morgan L. Sigel said Marsh's body was found by Mr. and Mrs. Richard Woods of Hinsdale, who were returning to their own car after a call at the funeral home. They discovered Marsh slumped behind the wheel after hearing a gasping sound from the parked car.

Dr. Percy C. Law of Cattaraugus, a county coroner, said Marsh lived for several minutes after he shot himself in the head with a .32 caliber rifle. The coroner issued a certificate of suicide.

Marsh was dressed in a freshly pressed dark blue suit. Beside his body was a note which read:

"I am sorry that I have to do this. Life without Sue is nothing."

On the car seat was a florist's box containing the spray of roses. On the box was written: "These roses are for Sue."

Sheriff Sigel identified Marsh as the man who had been found in Mrs. Riggs' closet early yesterday, touching off the argument which led to the shooting of the Little

Dept. at 2:07, just twelve minutes after he had come home, and reported he had just shot his wife.

Deputy Charles Donahue went to the complex home, three blocks from the sheriff's office, through a misunderstanding believed he was investigating only a domestic dispute. He saw a car leave the driveway and move around the block. He followed, and when the car returned to the driveway he went up to it and found Riggs on the floor inside, with the doors locked.

Donahue radioed for Sheriff Sigel, who drove to the Lodge and told Riggs covered while the deputy entered the lighted home.

He came out quickly and reported: "She's dead."

Says 'Daddy Shot Mommy'

He said when he entered the house, three-year-old Ralph Jr. met him and told him: "Daddy shot Mommy."

The deputy found Mrs. Riggs' body face up in a pool of blood on the boy's bed. Dr. James W. Tall, local physician, pronounced her dead, and Dr. James M. Happell of Salamanca, a county coroner, was summoned.

He ordered the body taken to the funeral home and later issued a certificate of homicide.

The sheriff's officers meanwhile forced Riggs from the car and took him into custody for questioning. Later they located Marsh and interrogated him.

Marsh was released after making statements to the investigators and agreeing to be on hand to testify before the grand jury to convene Monday in Supreme Court here.

Born April 9, 1932 on the East Randolph-Steamburg Rd. in the Town of Coldspring, Marsh had been employed as a milk-route driver by Dairyland of Little Valley the past three years.

Marsh was Star Athlete

Marsh was graduated from Randolph Central High School in 1950, and won an award as the school's "best all-around athlete" that year. During his high school career, he played three years of basketball, two years of football, and was a member of the Student Council three years.

Spread · **Austria**

Murder - Suicide

Chapter III. The Trial

Let's say I committed this crime, even if I did, it would have been because I loved her very much, right

— O.J. Simpson

She was my woman, as she deceived me I watched and went out of my mind.

— Tom Jones, "Delilah"

On the morning of January 18, 1957 Judge Philip J. Weiss carefully explained to the jury the legal definition of homicide and the possible extenuating circumstances, which might prevail in a murder case, including temporary insanity. He then charged the seven women and five men who would determine Ralph Riggs' immediate future to consider five possible verdicts: guilty of second degree murder, as charged, guilty of first degree manslaughter, guilty of second degree manslaughter, not guilty by reason of insanity, and not guilty. Given the facts of the case, which included Riggs' statement to the Sheriff on the day of the murder, a finding of not guilty was a virtual impossibility. Concerning his statement, Riggs said his recollection of giving and signing it was vague. "I didn't care what I signed. What I loved was gone, I had no reason to live" (*Salamanca Republican-Press,* 01/18/1957).

Chapter III. The Trial

It was Riggs himself who called the Sheriff's Department shortly after the 2 a.m. murder and said, "I'm crazy, but I shot my wife" (*Jamestown Post Journal*, 11/28/1956). Not guilty by reason of insanity, the defense offered by defense attorney Robert Fleischer, was tenable given Riggs' disjointed account of the shooting.

On the witness stand for four hours in his own defense yesterday afternoon, Riggs said he had "blacked out" at the time of the shooting and could recall only "nightmarish events" of what happened after he found Marsh in the closet (*Salamanca Republican-Press*, 01/18/1957).

He remembered scuffling with Marsh after discovering him and Sue saying, "Think of the children" (*Buffalo Courier Express*, 01/18/1957). Riggs did not dispute breaking the glass of the gun cabinet, but added,

I don't actually remember striking (the gun cabinet). My little boy said to me, "You didn't mean to shoot mama, did you?"

That made me wonder what I had done, made me aware that I had done something (01/18/1957).

Immediately following the completion of the prosecution's case, Fleischer moved to have the second degree murder indictment dismissed on the grounds of failure to prove a prima facie case (sufficient at first impression). He argued the prosecution failed to meet the standard required of the indictment that Riggs had "willfully, feloniously, and with design" caused the death of his wife (01/17/1957). Although this motion was denied, it seems to have influenced the jury.

A plea of not guilty by reason of mental defect (insanity) has three subcategories, one of which arguably applied to the defendant. Under normal circumstances Riggs would have been expected to conform his behavior to the requirements of the law. However, the circumstances he encountered when he entered his home the morning of the murder were extraordinary and sufficient for the jury to consider that Riggs was in a state of temporary insanity. This defense is also referred to as *irresistible impulse*.

The success of an *irresistible impulse* defense depends on the facts of the case. For example, assume that a child has been molested. If the child's mother shoots and kills the suspected molester, the mother could argue that she was so enraged by the violation of her child that she was unable to control her actions. The mother need not have been diagnosed as mentally ill. Rather, she would need to show that she was mentally ill at the time of the shooting, and that the illness impaired her self-control.

Irresistible impulse emerged as a defense in the nineteenth century, when psychoanalysts formulated the concept of moral insanity to describe the temporary inability of otherwise sane persons to resist criminal behavior. Courts began to recognize the condition as one that rendered conduct involuntary and therefore not suitable for punishment (*legal-dictionary*, 08/15/2016).

Fleischer laid the foundation for this defense during jury selection when he asked prospective jurors, "If the court charges you that there is a question of sanity at the time of the alleged crime will you give the defendant the benefit of that doubt" (*Salamanca Republican-Press*, 01/15/1957).

The jury deliberated for approximately seven hours, interrupted by lunch and dinner breaks. The differences in the possible sentences were considerable. Second degree murder, a Class-A felony, called for a minimum sentence of 20 years and maximum sentence of life imprisonment without parole. First degree or involuntary manslaughter, a Class-B felony, carried a maximum sentence of 20 years with no minimum sentence established. Second degree or voluntary manslaughter, a Class-C felony, called for a minimum sentence of three-and-a-half years and a maximum sentence of 15 years. Not guilty by reason of mental defect likely would have resulted in a sentence of mandatory psychiatric care.

At 11:12 p.m. jury foreman Fred Speedy announced, "We find the defendant guilty of first degree manslaughter" (*Jamestown Post Journal*, 01/19/1957). Given the option of second degree manslaughter and the defense provided by Fleischer, the jury's verdict seems somewhat enigmatic. In first degree manslaughter the victim's death is the unintended result of a negligent act. In second degree manslaughter the victim is killed under circumstances that would cause a reasonable person to be emotionally disturbed and temporarily incapable of conforming his behavior to the requirements of the law. Although second degree manslaughter called for a lesser maximum sentence compared to first degree manslaughter (20 years compared to 15 years), second degree manslaughter required a 3.5 year minimum sentence. First degree manslaughter had no minimum sentence, leaving this to Judge Weiss' discretion. This invites speculation that the jury was sympathetic to Riggs and did not want him to go to prison for at least three-and-a-half years and possibly they did not want him to go to prison at all. (The only surviving juror, Vivian Reithmiller, now 86-years-old, said she remembered only that she was a juror but could recall nothing concerning the deliberations.)

Riggs appeared "calm and unemotional" after hearing the verdict (01/19/1957). Fleischer requested a meeting with Judge Weiss to present a "special motion" to be considered before sentencing (01/19/1957). The request was granted. The content of this motion is not known but it was effective. Riggs received a sentence of one-year imprisonment and three years probation. A reasonable inference from the verdict and sentence is the jury and Judge Weiss saw Ralph Riggs as a man who murdered but was not a wanton murderer. They wrestled with the question of appropriate punishment and determined the circumstances drove him do something he would not have done otherwise.

In *Out of Character*, psychologists David DeSteno and Pierrecarlo Valdesolo address two competing theories of moral conduct. The *trait theory* posits each of us has characteristics that do not vary according to mood or circumstance. Hence, our moral conduct is predictable. The *variable theory* asserts that each of us is influenced by mood and circumstance sufficiently to make our behavior unpredictable (2011, p. 219). DeSteno and Valdesolo

26

expressed agreement with the variable theory when they wrote:

> Should a single moral failing erase a lifetime of good behavior? Why does a single transgression seem to give us license to brand someone with the indelible mark of a marred character? One explanation is that because these single events are so shocking and so memorable (not to mention so beaten to death by the media), they eclipse all else (p. 7).

It seems the jury and Judge Weiss viewed Riggs through the lens of the variable theory. However, this is not the only lens through which Ralph Riggs could be viewed. Ben-Zeev believes there is a "simplicity of prevailing views (that) evades the question of why certain men murder their wives" (2014, p. 2). Accordingly, he has written:

> (W)ife murder cannot be understood in terms of loss of control or local insanity. It is rather a deliberate act, which is the result of emotional ripeness that created mental readiness for committing the murder as an act of profound despair that is ready to destroy the other even if this means destroying oneself (p. 2).

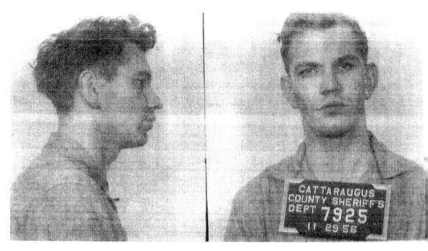

Ralph Riggs's arrest/booking

Chapter IV. The Aftermath

The Lord...lays the sins of the parents upon their children; the entire family is affected - even children in the third and fourth generations.

-Numbers 14:18

The "ripple effect" is the concept that every action, great or small, has far reaching repercussions. The metaphor often used to communicate this idea is that of a pebble thrown into a pond that produces concentric waves emanating from the point of the pebble's impact. The principle that a seemingly inconsequential cause can have unpredictable, innumerable effects is referred to in the scientific community as the "butterfly effect." If small events reverberate well beyond themselves, what are the consequences of great events, like murders and suicides?

Concerning suicide, the controversial psychiatrist Thomas Szasz posited:

Suicide is a fundamental human right. That does not mean that it is morally desirable. It only means that society does not have the moral right to interfere, by force, with a person's decision to commit this act (1973, p. 67).

The premise of his analysis is each person's life is her own possession. But this premise is questionable, if not flawed. Except for the few hermits among us, no one lives a life that has no effect on others.

Suicide is described as an impersonal act, yet it kills a part of everyone who is close to or loves the person who dies. The emotional pain for the suicide victim is over, but it is only beginning for the survivors (Smith, 1986, p. 85).

The number of suicide survivors is considerable. Edwin Shneidman, the eminent psychologist quoted in chapter two, offered this estimate:

If there are 50,000 committed suicides in the United States each year – not counting the couple million "subintentioned" presently labeled natural, and homicidal deaths – then there are at least 200,000 survivor-victims created each year whose lives are forever benighted by the event (1972, pp. x-xi).

This 4:1 ratio applies to the suicide of Albert Marsh, Jr. He left behind three children and an ex-wife, all affected by his death, albeit in different ways. Shneidman characterized survivor-victims with an aphorism well known to mental health professionals: "The person who commits suicide puts his psychological skeleton in the survivor's emotional closet" (1988, p. x).

Ironic is both Albert and Ralph perceived Sue Ann as his whole world. According to Ben Zeev this perception has consequences: "The man perceives the woman to be his whole world so that he feels any separation from her entails a loss of his own identity" (2014, p. 4). In Albert's case, his life lacked "other sources of meaning and reasons for living" (p. 4). In Ralph's case, his,

> traditional perception of masculinity, which dictates that the male has full power, honor, and control, runs counter to his dependency upon his wife, making that reliance appear evidence of his weakness and humiliation, and an affront to masculine honor (p. 4).

Ralph conforms to the psychodynamic explanation for uxoricide, which features unconscious conflict:

(M)en who kill their partners experience both an unconscious dependence on their wife and a resentment of her. These men wish to leave the relationship, but unknowingly perceive themselves as too helpless to do so, which culminates in a belief that killing the wife is the only way to be free of her (Cormier, 1982).

Implications for the Children

The Campbell Study, published in 2007, reported children were home in 65 percent of cases of uxoricide and 43 percent witnessed the homicide (Hardesty, 2007). Children who have lost one parent at the hands of the other, almost always the father, in effect lose both parents. Often the children are taken to live with a grandmother, usually the mother of the murder victim (Steeves, 2003). This was the case in the Riggs uxoricide until Ralph was released from prison. Following his release he acquired custody of two of his children and eventually remarried (The youngest, Mary, was taken by Sue Ann's brother and his wife who relocated several times in different states to prevent Mary's return to her father.)

Interview with Ralph, Now Age 63

This interview was conducted in the summer of 2016, 60 years after the murder of his mother.

Questions: Regarding your sisters:

- What have they said about your mother's murder?
- What have they said about how it affected them?
- How do they feel about both your mother and father?

Ralph: Kris and I have talked about our mother's death quite often since we were old enough to understand what we were talking about. That discussion was in hushed tones when we were young, as the subject was taboo in the household following our father's remarriage. We were to refer to our stepmother as our mother and we never talked about our real mother at all.

Kris has always tended toward blaming our mother for her creating the circumstances resulting in her death by having been unfaithful. She tends to look for ways to, if not excuse our father, at least understand his actions and sympathize with his guilt, shame and remorse. Bear in mind that she and I lived together with our father for a few years between his release from prison and his remarriage. During that period we were allowed to spend significant time with our maternal grandmother and that side of the family. That "privilege" was taken away around 1960.

We never saw much of our sister Mary growing up, as she was taken by my mother's brother, John, immediately following our mother's death. She grew up among the side of the family that held an ever-present animosity toward our father. I have legal documents from their unsuccessful efforts to have parental rights for her as well Kris and me terminated from our father so they could adopt us all. Since our father tried through the legal system to force them to return her custody to him, they moved to several different states while she was growing up, each time changing jurisdictions. Eventually our father abandoned that effort. Later, at Kris's urging, he made contact with Mary after she grew into adulthood. I do not know at what age she was told she was adopted, but I believe it was in early adolescence. She is not inclined to engage in these discussions at all. I gave her a copy of the set of documents I shared with you and she has never had much to say to me about it.

Growing up I don't think Kris felt our mother's absence as much as I, but she was abused more severely than I by our stepmother.

Question: Did your father ever express to you regret or

guilt or both concerning what he did?

Ralph: Yes, on two occasions, one when I was 15 and had run away from home a second time. I had left a letter in which I said, among other things, that if he could get away with killing my mother I should be able to get away with running away from that household. He sat down with me and went over the letter point by point. I don't remember exactly what else I had written, except that it was full of inept cursing and vulgarity. He said that he did not "get away" with killing my mother. I think he tried as best he could to explain his actions to an angry 15-year-old. As the angry 15-year-old, I did my best to disregard everything he was saying, but obviously something stuck, as I do remember him making the attempt. The other time, I was in my 20's. He and I went drinking and we wound up in a bar in Little Valley. We had quite a long talk about it, and I remember him saying "I (meaning he) over-reacted" and "Your mother was an angel. She had one fault." which I presume he meant, men.

Question: What do your children know about your mother's murder?

Ralph: They both knew growing up that my mother died

when I was very young. They did not know of all the details until they were adults. My daughter once told me that in a college class she took they were asked to describe a personal hero and she described me. My son used my "sad story" and recovery from alcohol abuse in a paper describing his own decision not to drink or use drugs. Both these things heighten my shame and remorse and I hope someday I can be their hero again.

Question: What do you think of this quotation?

"We all get damned in our lives, and there are ripple effects. One thing can determine a life, and it's hard to overcome that if the event is really traumatic. Your life is completely condemned by it." (Matthias Schoenaerts, actor)

Ralph: Hardly a day goes by when I don't think about the loss of my mother. I have felt deprived of her love and support yet toughened by that deprivation. I recently heard it put that PTSD is not a refusal to let go of the past, it's the past refusing to let go of you. Everyone experiences trauma or tragedy in one form or another. People tend to empathize more when the event happens to children, but I think children tend to be much more resilient and capable of coming to terms with harsh realities than they are often given credit for, and that we in this culture tend to try to shield them from such things. But tragedy and trauma happen to everyone. I think the ripple effects speak to our interconnectedness.

I think overcoming trauma means achieving balance between reason/rationality and emotion. To do that you have to face and learn how to live with the anguish, the rage, the unfairness and irrationality and come to an understanding that with great trauma comes great gifts. But to get at the gift, you have to work to polish and hone the jagged edges. It can take a long time, it takes a lot of help and sometimes the help isn't gentle or caring. If you can get to that balance, you may find your tragedy was a gift, and that your gift is for you to give back to the world, giving high purpose and meaning to your life.

Question: What was it like growing up in a small town with the notoriety of you being the boy whose father murdered his mother?

Ralph: I always sensed being the center of attention, but from a distance. There was a huge "elephant in the room" that people were always whispering about but nobody would talk about to me. My sister Kris and I didn't even talk to each other

37

about it until we were well into grade school. As I grew older, it slowly dawned on me that even with the various school systems we were in, as we moved around the southern tier of NY, I was at least a curiosity. Since my grandmother was a schoolteacher and was well connected in that community, Kris and I would encounter people who would say they knew my grandmother, which was kind of code for saying they knew about the way my mother died. I assume now that they also had an idea that I had witnessed her death, although I was never completely assured of the truth of that, or what other people understood about it, until I took it on myself to investigate and verify whether or not what I remembered was accurate. So I guess I learned not to talk about important things, maybe that raw emotion is dangerous. I think I also learned not to be sure of myself. My sense of what was true and not true, right and wrong, was somewhat fluid or tenuous. I was in my 40's before I decided I wanted to know what really happened, if my memory served me well, and started to dig into what sources of information were available. I wish I had done that sooner in life and had the opportunity to talk with some of the people from outside the family, who would not have that perspective of one "camp" or the other and who could possibly have helped me achieve something approaching equilibrium in my thinking and feelings about the event.

As I grew, I became jealous and resentful toward other kids who had what I perceived as wholesome, supportive families. I think this was as much a result of the clear signals coming from my stepmother that Kris and I were welcome in her home only until they were no longer legally required to provide for us. As I began to encounter problems with authority and incur disciplinary action, I developed the internal antisocial rationalization that "I watched my father shoot my mother dead while she was holding me when I was three, so what do you think you're going to do to me that's going to bother me?" It was a pretty unhealthy way to think about things. Maybe it served some purpose at the time, but it played into a sentiment of having been robbed of a mother's love and nurturing, therefore any antisocial behavior was justified. I didn't have to live by society's rules.

Question: Have you ever wondered, as the son of a man who committed murder, if that capability is in you?

Ralph: I did for a time, but since we moved frequently growing up I had to deal with bullies a lot. At first I ran from them or got beat up. At some point I learned to tap into the rage I have always carried and learned, if not to fight from a martial skill perspective, at least to explode unpredictably so people would leave me alone. A part of me wanted to know how I would behave in combat, which was a reason I enlisted at age 17 during Vietnam and volunteered to go there. Fortunately or not, I was not assigned to a combat role, but was close enough to the war to have gained a sense of the industrial scale death and destruction that is war. Later, as I progressed into a lifestyle of drinking and drug use, I made a point not to acquire a handgun, though I did carry a shotgun in my truck and frequently a large knife on my person.

I still struggle with rage, mostly inwardly, but have not been in a physical fight since I quit drinking over 33 years ago. Somewhere between then and now, as I began to learn about chronic anger, I learned of the difference between "hot anger" and "cold, hard anger," which can lead to hate and toward evil. I believe at one time it was possible for me to have become an assassin, like (serial murderer Richard) Klukinski, the fellow you reference in one of your books.

Question: Do you think your father lied at his trial? (Especially his claim that he didn't remember shooting your mother.)

Ralph: I don't know. I have asked myself that question and have tried to answer truthfully. I have tended to want to think not, but I wonder if he made the initial call to the police, then realized, after talking to a lawyer, that he should not have made the admissions he did and so adjusted his story to fit the requirements of the legal argument they made. I also wonder if he did not "set them (my mother and Albert Marsh) up" by saying he would not be home, then coming home anyway. If I just go by my understanding of human character, I believe my father tried to be a fundamentally honest person in his life. He made a huge mistake, for which he suffered the rest of his life. He had flaws, a temper, he liked to drink, he was a bit of a flirt around other women, particularly when he was drinking. ... I've been told that I "bonded" with my father, that he was a fundamentally bad person and that my judgment is flawed. I supposed that's possible, but I have to go by my own sense of this. So I'll say that he told the truth as he saw it, he made a mistake he wished for the rest of his life that he had not made, and the consequences of that mistake at that time were not what they might have been today.

Interview with Kristie Yunker, now Age 61, conducted in the fall of 2016.

Chapter IV. The Aftermath

Question: How do you feel about your parents?

Kristie: How did I feel about my parents? That's a complicated question. I loved my dad, deeply, once I came to know him again. When he was imprisoned, we lived with our grandmother, and I had only happy memories of those years, when I was between the ages of a year-and-a-half and four. We were surrounded by loving relatives and our grandmother was a kind person, who, despite her own grief, showered us with love and attention, even as she worked full time as a teacher in Little Valley. I can't remember ever talking about my parents with her when I was little - I didn't even know that they existed - until the day came when we all went to the courthouse for a custody hearing. Our dad wanted us back, and our grandmother didn't want to give us up.

I remember this strange man and my grandmother on the witness stand, each of them crying while giving testimony, and being only four years old, I wasn't able to understand what was going on. But then, the hearing ended and Ralph and I were torn from the arms of our grandmother and given to our father. My grandmother, her sisters and their husbands were crying, so we knew this was not a good thing. We were driven to Portville, about an hour away, I think, to live with my father's lifelong friend, Bob Ide and his family. Ralph and I visited with Mr. Ide a few years ago and he told me that I screamed for the entire drive until they stopped for ice cream. Ralph started kindergarten there and I roamed about the Ide's rural property alone; that's when my imaginary friend appeared (and only there - he didn't "come with us" when we moved away). Ralph and I had lost our parents, then our grandmother, then we were given back to our father (whom we didn't know). The Ide's (who were no relation to us and who we didn't know) let us live with them for a few months. Then it was on to our paternal grandmother (who was NOT a warm person) and finally we arrived in the home of our step-mother. It was traumatic.

Our family never, ever discussed the topic of my parents with us nor with their own four children. I asked my dad about it one time, a year or two before he died, when we were alone in the car driving to my grandmother's (where I was staying for a week), after leaving my sister, Mary's house. (Dad had come to know her and her family only a few years previous to that time.) I asked him what had happened between him and my mother, telling him that I knew the basic story, but I wanted to hear it from his perspective. He said, "Oh, it would take me a case of beer to tell you this story. I can't do it." I was angry at his response, and said that it would be wrong for him to take it to his grave. He wouldn't budge, and he did do just that - took it to his grave. He was able to talk to Ralph about it - over alcohol - but his guilt and his grief prevented him from discussing it with me, I think.

My sister Mary is conflicted in her feelings about both our parents, but she was raised by our mother's brother, who never got over what had happened to his only sibling, and who often expressed hatred for our father, and elevated his sister to sainthood status. I did talk to my step-mother about it, however, just a couple of years ago. Ralph had been helping her deal with her sister's estate, and he and I talked about how "clueless" she was about how we felt as children. I think that during her visit back east, he wanted to clear the air with her, but she didn't want to deal with his feelings. I was angry at her response to his reaching out. I've always been protective about my brother, and decided to write to her and tell her that Ralph was deeply affected by the murder etc. The revelation that we KNEW the story seemed to come as a shock to her, and she called me after receiving my letter. For the first time, at the age of 58, I talked with my step-mother about what had happened to my father's first wife. She said that she and Dad had wanted to bury the secret, not tell any of the children (including us - not knowing that one of us remembered it vividly), and to "start new lives, putting that behind" them. To this day, she has never told my adult half-siblings and I have taken it upon myself to tell two of them. I think they deserve to know. When my own children became adults, I told them too.

I learned the story of our parents initially from Ralph, who told me when I was around 5 that our father had killed our mother, and that we had a little sister somewhere in the world. I didn't believe him, not really - I couldn't imagine this man killing anyone - not this man who held me and read to me at night, who laughed at my antics (I was the family entertainer), and who played with us when he wasn't working, But while I was spending a week with my paternal grandmother, I came upon some newspaper clippings that she had saved that told the story of the event and the trial. I was somewhere between 8 and 10 years old by then, and I read that my father had, in fact, killed my mother in a jealous rage. I read what he said when he was arrested - that he had "three reasons to live - his children", and I read the headlines that trumpeted the story of the "love triangle". I blamed her, not him, for what had happened. How could she be having an affair while our father was working? How could she be having sex with someone while her three children, one a BABY, were asleep just feet away in their beds?

I saw my father in a new light – I viewed him then as a tortured man, who grieved for what had happened, who drank too much because of that grief, and who had married the second time in haste, looking for a mother for his children. In later years, I think he came to regret that marriage as he saw that our step-mother had driven Ralph from our home, and who treated me unfairly over her own children. I remember an argument the two of them had one late night when I was around 12, when, through the walls that separated our rooms, I heard her say, "You favor her because she looks like her mother!" He answered that it wasn't true. She said something in a lower voice that I couldn't hear, and then he said, "I could KILL you!" At that point, knowing that he was capable of doing such a thing, I leaped up and ran to their room, bursting in, and crying, "No Dad! Don't kill her!" I was escorted back to my room. I'm not sure what they made of that.

As I matured, I saw things from a different perspective. As a young mother whose husband worked on the pipeline and was thus away from our home for two weeks of every month, I understood how my own mother, young and vibrant, might have felt. She might have felt abandoned, disillusioned by an unhappy marriage, and longing for the love and attention of a lover, she might have reached out to Mr. Marsh. I made a vow to myself (along with my marriage vows) that I would never do such a thing - not to my husband, and certainly not to my children. I would not be that person. But I began to see how

46

she might have felt, and I began to feel compassion for her that I had not experienced before.

Question: What do you think about your father's sentence?

Kristie: I didn't turn up any information about why my father's sentence was so light. I guess I always felt that in those years, a man could be easily forgiven for acting in a crime of passion when his wife was clearly cheating on him. I read once that until 1972, Texas law allowed a man who caught his wife in bed with another man was justified in killing both! Maybe that was the general feeling, if not the law, in other states during the 50's, too.

Question: Do you know how your mother and Albert Marsh met?

Kristie: I don't know how my mother and Albert Marsh met, but since Little Valley and Randolph are only about 12 miles apart, it's not hard to imagine that they met at a football/basketball/baseball game between their schools. My mother was also a competitive speed skater - was Marsh?

My mother's cousin, Howard Nuttall, who is now deceased, told me that Marsh was my mother's high school boyfriend, before she met my father, and that my grandmother disapproved of him because he didn't seem to be a "good catch". Gram very much approved of my father, who was a college graduate and had a bright future before him. My parents apparently met when my father was working on a road project in Cattaraugus County, and they had a brief courtship before my mother found herself pregnant with my brother. They were married six months before Ralph was born.

Question: Do you know anything about Albert Marsh's ex-wife and children?

Kristie: I don't know why Marsh's wife left and why she didn't take the children is a question I've always wondered about too. I don't know how long my mother and Marsh's affair had been going on - you mentioned the times that my father caught them together - but it could be that they never really got over one another, and Marsh's wife knew that.

Question: Regarding the loss of your mother, do you think you are different from Ralph and Mary?

Kristie: All three of us feel that our lives were irreparably damaged by the event. Our childhoods were unhappy on many levels, and Mary's wasn't happy, either. I believe that we are all products, not only of our genetics, but of our experiences in life, and of the nurturing we received as children. Some of us are blessed with the gifts of resiliency and empathy that shield us from suffering needlessly from pain incurred decades ago, and that give us the ability to understand multiple points of view, which then allows us to forgive. I think that I am blessed in that way, but that Ralph, and to a lesser degree, Mary, have issues with "the event" that they wrestle with to this day. Did the fact that they both lived in Little Valley and the nearby area for most of their lives cause them to be unable to forgive and forget? I moved away from the area when I was 17 - maybe that gives me an advantage. I'll leave that question to you.

I am curious to know more about the people involved, but I harbor no hatred for any of the three people in "the triangle" - it has never occurred to me to blame Marsh, by the way. To me, he was incidental to their troubled marriage, his death a tragic loss for his family. There was our tragedy, and there was his. The tragedies of the deaths were separate in the impact they had on their respective families.

Question: From reading my account of your mother's murder and Albert Marsh's suicide (chapters I – III) were you surprised by anything you read?

Kristie: What you have written thus far corresponds with what I've read, and there were only a couple of surprises, or perhaps details I had forgotten. They are: I assumed that Dad left us alone in the room with our deceased mother; I didn't know that he took us back to bed afterward. I am relieved to know this for some reason. I knew that Dad waited in the car for the Sheriff to arrive; I didn't realize that he had driven around the block and returned to the house to await the police. This seems to me to point to his state of alcohol-induced confusion, and to his realization that he should face a moral reckoning for his actions.

JAMESTOWN, N.Y., THURSDAY, NOVEMBER 29, 1956

MURDER AND SUICIDE CLIMAXES MARITAL TRIANGLE — Above photo shows modest two-story house in Little Valley where Mrs. Sue Ann Riggs, (inset) 24-year-old mother of three children was shot to death early Wednesday morning when her husband Ralph (left) came home and found a man in the bed room. The man, later identified as Albert Marsh, Jr., 24, a milk delivery man, committed suicide in a car parked outside the funeral home where Mrs. Riggs' body had been taken. For these photos turn to Page 27

—Post-Journal Staff foto

Ralph and Sue Ann Riggs

51

References

Introduction

Peck, M. Scott. (1983). *The people of the lie: The hope for healing human evil.* New York: Simon and Schuster.

Donne, J. (1624). "No man is an island." *Meditation XVII.* Recovered from PoemHunter.com on 07/11/2016.

Chapter I. The Murder

Marsh. A. Statement made to Sheriff Morgan Sigel, State of New York, County of Cattaraugus, Village of Little Valley on November 28, 1956.

Mongillo, J. Report of 8:12 p.m. on 09/04/54. Cattaraugus County Sheriff's Department. Nature of Complaint: "Family Trouble."

Riggs, R. Statement made to Sheriff Morgan Sigel, State of New York, County of Cattaraugus, Village of Little Valley on November 28, 1956.

Viorst, J. (1986). *Necessary losses: The loves, illusions, dependencies, and impossible expectations that all of us have to give up in order to grow.* New York: Fireside.

Chapter II. The Suicide

Ben-Zeev, A. (2014). "Why do (some) men murder the wives they love? Is killing out of love possible." *Psychology Today.* September 22, 2014.

References

Jamison, K. (1999). *Night falls fast: Understanding suicide.* New York: Alfred A. Knopf.

Karr, M. (2001). *Viper rum.* New York: Penguin Group.

Maltsberger, J. (1987). Keynote address at the Annual Meeting of the American Association of Suicidologists at the Copley Plaza in Boston, MA.

Shneidman, E. (1996). *The suicidal mind.* New York: Oxford University Press.

Chapter III. The Trial

Ben-Zeev, A. (2014). "Why do (some) men murder the wives they love? Is killing out of love possible." *Psychology Today.* September 22, 2014.

Buffalo Courier-Express. "Vague on fatal shooting of wife, Riggs tells jury." Friday, 01/18/1957.

DeSteno, D. and Valdesolo, P. (2011). *Out of character: Surprising truths about the liar, cheat, sinner (and saint) in all of us.* New York: Random House.

Jamestown Post Journal. "Mother of 3 killed in Little Valley. Wednesday, 11/28/1956.

_____ . "Jury finds Riggs guilty on manslaughter count." Thursday, 01/19/1957.

legal dictionary www.http://legaldictionary.thefreedictionary .com /Irresistible+Impulse. Recovered on 08/15/2016.

Salamanca Republican Press. "Jury is deliberating in Riggs murder trial." Friday, 01/18/1957.

_____. "Riggs to testify; case completed by prosecution." Thursday, 01/17/1957.

_____. "Four jurors are seated as Riggs trial opens." Tuesday, 01/15/1957.

Chapter IV. The Aftermath

Ben-Zeev, A. (2014). "Why do (some) men murder the wives they love? Is killing out of love possible." *Psychology Today.* September 22, 2014.

Cormier, B.M. (1982). "Psychodynamics of homicide committed in a marital relationship." *Corrective Psychiatry and Journal of Social Therapy.* 8:114-118.

Hardesty J.L., Campbell J.C., McFarlane J.M., & Lewandowski L.A. "How children and their caregivers adjust after intimate partner femicide." *Journal of Family Issues.* 2007: 29:100–24.

Shneidman, E. (1972). Survivors of suicide. Albert C. Cain, Editor. Springfield, IL: Charles C. Thomas.

_____. (1988). *The encyclopedia of suicide, first edition. New York: Facts on File.*

Smith, J. (1986). *Survivors of suicide.* New York: The Rosen Publishing Group.

Steeves, R. (2003). *"Children of uxoricide." Emotional abuse and faith.* 06/03/2003.

References

Szasz, T. (1973). *The second sin.* New York: Doubleday and Company.

About the Author

Max Malikow is on the faculty of the Renee Crown Honors Program of Syracuse University and an Adjunct Assistant Professor of Philosophy at LeMoyne College. He earned his Master's degree from Gordon-Conwell Theological Seminary and Doctorate from Boston University. The author of twelve previous books, he is a practicing psychotherapist in Syracuse, New York.

Made in the USA
Middletown, DE
08 August 2019